CONTENTS

Introduction
Advertisement for a Restaurant	1
Advertisement for a School	3
Advertisement for a Holiday resort	5
Advertisement for a Hospital	7
Advertisement for a Salon	9
Advertisement for a Burger shop	11
Advertisement for a Grocery shop	12
Advertisement for a Book store	14
Advertisement for a Bakery	16
Advertisement for a Supermarket	17
Advertisement for a Mall	19
Advertisement for a Theater	21
Advertisement for a Cinema hall	23
Advertisement for a Toy store	25
Advertisement for a Fun zone	27
Should students be required to wear uniforms in school?	30
Should students be required to wear uniforms in school?	32
Should homework be banned in schools?	34
Should homework be banned in schools?	36
Should all students be required to learn a second language in	38

school?	
Should all students be required to learn a second language in school?	40
Should parents limit their children's screen time?	42
Should parents limit their children's screen time?	44
Should there be examinations in school?	46
Should there be examinations in school?	48
Should schools have longer recess periods?	50
Should schools have longer recess periods?	52
Should eating chocolates be banned from school premises?	54
Should eating chocolates be banned from school premises?	56

INTRODUCTION

Writing persuasive texts involves convincing your audience to adopt your point of view or take specific action. Here are some tips to help you write persuasive text effectively:

Start with a clear thesis statement.

Your thesis statement should be a concise statement of your argument or position. It should be placed at the beginning of your text and provide a clear focus for the rest of your writing.

Example: Thesis statement: The government should ban plastic bags to reduce environmental damage.

Use persuasive language.

Use language that is compelling and convincing. Avoid overly technical or academic language that can be difficult for your audience to understand. Use strong, active verbs and avoid using passive voice.

Example: The indiscriminate use of plastic bags is a threat to our environment. It is time to take action and make a change to protect our planet.

Use evidence to support your argument

Use statistics, facts, and examples to support your

argument. Provide evidence that is relevant and reliable.

Example: According to a study by the World Wildlife Fund, approximately 10% of plastic waste ends up in the ocean, harming marine life and polluting our water. In addition, plastic bags can take up to 1,000 years to decompose, contributing to landfill overflow.

Consider your audience

Understand your audience's perspective and anticipate their objections. Address their concerns in your writing and provide counterarguments.

Example: I understand that some people argue that plastic bags are convenient and inexpensive. However, the cost to our environment and our health is too high to ignore.

Use rhetorical devices

Use rhetorical devices like repetition, alliteration, and metaphor to make your writing more memorable and engaging.

Example: Plastic bags are not only a problem, they are a plague. They are suffocating our oceans and killing marine life. It is time to say no to plastic bags and yes to a healthier planet.

Appeal to emotions

Use emotional appeals to create a connection with your audience.

Example: Imagine a world where our oceans are clean and our marine life is thriving. By banning plastic bags, we can make this dream a reality. Let's take action now to protect our planet and secure a better future for ourselves and future generations.

There are different types of persuasive writing. In this book, I will provide examples of mainly two types of persuasive writing:

1) Advertisements
   Advertisements are persuasive texts that aim to convince the audience to purchase a product or service. They often use emotional appeals and persuasive language to make a sale.
2) Argumentative writing
   This type of writing presents a well-reasoned argument in favor of a particular viewpoint. It often includes a counter-argument and refutation of opposing viewpoints.

ADVERTISEMENTS

ADVERTISEMENT FOR A RESTAURANT

Are you looking for an unforgettable dining experience? Look no further than our restaurant!

From the moment you step through our doors, you'll be transported to a world of culinary delight. Our chefs are dedicated to crafting dishes that are not only visually stunning but also bursting with flavor. We use only the freshest, highest-quality ingredients to create dishes that will tantalize your taste buds.

But it's not just the food that sets us apart. Our restaurant is designed to be a feast for the senses. The ambiance is warm and inviting, with soft lighting and comfortable seating. You'll be surrounded by beautiful decor that complements the delicious food.

Our staff is dedicated to providing exceptional service. From the moment you arrive, you'll be treated like royalty. We believe that dining out should be a special experience, and we're committed to making sure that every guest who walks through our doors feels pampered and well-cared for.

Whether you're celebrating a special occasion or simply looking for a night out, our restaurant is the perfect choice. We offer a wide range of menu options to suit any taste, from vegetarian and gluten-free options to hearty meat dishes. And of course, we have an extensive selection of wines, cocktails, and other beverages to complement your meal.

So what are you waiting for? Come dine with us and discover what makes our restaurant so special. We're confident that once you experience the flavors, ambiance, and service we offer, you'll be back for more.

ADVERTISEMENT FOR A SCHOOL

As parents, choosing the right school for your child is one of the most important decisions you'll ever make. That's why we believe that our school is the best choice for your child's education.

Our school is more than just a place where children come to learn. We are a community of educators, students, and families who are all committed to ensuring that every child reaches their full potential. Our curriculum is designed to challenge and inspire students, while also providing them with the tools and resources they need to succeed.

We believe in a holistic approach to education, which means that we focus on the whole child - not just their academic achievements. Our teachers are dedicated to providing a nurturing and supportive environment that encourages creativity, exploration, and critical thinking. We also offer a range of extracurricular activities, including sports, music, drama, and more, to help students develop their interests and talents outside of the classroom.

At our school, we believe that every child has the potential to make a difference in the world. We strive to instill in our students a sense of social responsibility and a commitment to making positive change. We encourage our students to think beyond themselves and to become active members of their communities.

We also believe that education is a partnership between the school and parents. We are committed to keeping parents informed and involved in their child's education. We offer regular communication, parent-teacher conferences, and other opportunities for parents to be engaged in their child's learning journey.

Choosing the right school for your child is an important decision, and we understand that there are many options to consider. But we believe that our school offers the best education and experience for your child. Come visit us and see for yourself why our school is the right choice for your family.

ADVERTISEMENT FOR A HOLIDAY RESORT

Are you in need of a luxurious and relaxing getaway? Look no further than our resorts!

Our resorts are designed to be a haven from the stresses of everyday life. From the moment you arrive, you'll be transported to a world of indulgence and relaxation. We offer a range of accommodations to suit any preference, from cozy rooms to spacious villas.

But it's not just the accommodations that set us apart. Our resorts offer a wide range of amenities and activities to ensure that your stay is unforgettable. Whether you want to lounge by the pool, indulge in a spa treatment, or explore the surrounding area, we have something for everyone.

Our restaurants are staffed by top chefs who are dedicated to creating dishes that are as visually stunning as they are delicious. We use only the freshest, highest-quality ingredients to ensure that every meal is a culinary delight.

We also offer a range of activities to keep you entertained during your stay. Whether you're looking for adventure or relaxation, our resorts have something for everyone. From water sports and golf to yoga and meditation, we have activities to suit every interest and skill level.

Our staff is dedicated to providing exceptional service to ensure that your stay is stress-free and enjoyable. We believe that every guest deserves to be treated like royalty, and we are committed to making sure that every aspect of your stay is perfect.

So why wait? Book your stay at one of our resorts today and experience the ultimate in luxury and relaxation. We're confident that once you experience the amenities, activities, and service we offer, you'll be back for more.

ADVERTISEMENT FOR A HOSPITAL

When it comes to healthcare, you want the very best for yourself and your loved ones. That's why we believe that our hospital is the right choice for all of your medical needs.

Our hospital is staffed by highly skilled and compassionate healthcare professionals who are dedicated to providing exceptional care to every patient. We have state-of-the-art facilities and equipment, as well as the latest medical technology to ensure that we can provide the best possible care to our patients.

We understand that being in the hospital can be stressful and overwhelming. That's why we've designed our facilities to be as comfortable and welcoming as possible. We offer private rooms with comfortable beds and modern amenities to help you feel at home.

Our staff is committed to providing personalized care that is tailored to your individual needs. We believe that every patient is unique, and we take the time to listen to your concerns and answer your questions. We work closely with you to develop a treatment plan that meets your needs and helps you achieve the best possible outcomes.

In addition to our medical services, we also offer a range of support services to help you during your stay. We have social workers, chaplains, and other specialists who are available to provide emotional support and guidance.

At our hospital, we believe that healthcare is a partnership between the patient and their healthcare providers. We are committed to keeping you informed and involved in your care every step of the way.

Choosing the right hospital for your medical needs is an important decision. We believe that our hospital offers the best possible care, service, and amenities to ensure that you receive the care you need and deserve. Come visit us and see for yourself why our hospital is the right choice for you and your loved ones.

ADVERTISEMENT FOR A SALON

Are you looking for a way to enhance your natural beauty and boost your confidence? Look no further than our salon!

Our salon is staffed by experienced and talented beauty professionals who are dedicated to providing exceptional service to every client. We offer a wide range of services, from hair styling and coloring to nail care and skincare.

We understand that everyone's beauty needs are unique. That's why we work closely with each client to understand their goals and preferences. We take the time to listen to your needs and provide personalized service that is tailored to your individual needs.

Our salon uses only the highest-quality products to ensure that our clients receive the best possible results. We are committed to using eco-friendly, natural, and organic products whenever possible to minimize the impact on the environment and ensure the safety of our clients.

In addition to our exceptional beauty services, we offer a range of amenities to help you relax and unwind during your visit. Our salon is designed to be a sanctuary from the stresses of everyday life. We offer comfortable seating, calming music, and a relaxing atmosphere to help you feel pampered and rejuvenated.

At our salon, we believe that beauty is about more than just looking good. It's about feeling confident and empowered in your own skin. We are committed to helping our clients achieve their beauty goals and feel their best every day.

Choosing the right salon for your beauty needs is an important decision. We believe that our salon offers the best possible service, quality, and results to ensure that you leave feeling beautiful, confident, and rejuvenated. Come visit us and see for yourself why our salon is the right choice for you.

ADVERTISEMENT FOR A BURGER SHOP

Looking for a burger that's more than just your average fast-food fare? Look no further than our burger shop!

Our burgers are made with only the highest-quality ingredients, from 100% pure beef patties to fresh, locally-sourced produce. We're committed to using only the freshest, most flavorful ingredients to ensure that every burger is a mouthwatering masterpiece.

But it's not just the ingredients that make our burgers special. We also offer a range of unique and creative toppings and sauces, from classic bacon and cheese to adventurous options like avocado and spicy aioli. And with our customizable options, you can create a burger that's perfectly suited to your tastes and preferences.

In addition to our delicious burgers, we also offer a range of sides and drinks to complete your meal. From crispy fries to refreshing shakes, we've got everything you need to satisfy your cravings.

At our burger shop, we believe that food should be more than just fuel for your body. It should be a delicious and enjoyable experience that leaves you feeling satisfied and happy. That's why we're committed to providing exceptional service and a welcoming, friendly atmosphere that makes you feel right at home.

So why settle for a boring, generic burger when you can have a delicious, gourmet masterpiece at our burger shop? Come visit us today and see for yourself why we're the best burger joint in town!

ADVERTISEMENT FOR A GROCERY SHOP

Looking for a one-stop-shop for all your grocery needs? Look no further than our grocery store!

Our grocery store is the perfect place to stock up on everything from fresh produce and meats to pantry staples and household essentials. We offer a wide selection of high-quality products at affordable prices, making it easy to fill your cart without breaking the bank.

But it's not just the great prices that make our grocery store special. We're committed to providing a shopping experience that's convenient, enjoyable, and stress-free. From our friendly and knowledgeable staff to our well-organized aisles and easy-to-navigate layout, we've designed our store with the customer in mind.

And with our commitment to quality and freshness, you can feel good about the products you're buying. We work closely with local suppliers and farmers to ensure that our produce is always fresh and in-season, and we're constantly sourcing new and exciting products to add to our shelves.

At our grocery store, we believe that shopping for food should be a pleasurable and rewarding experience. That's why we offer a range of services and amenities to make your visit as enjoyable as possible, including in-store delis, bakeries, and cafes, as well as online ordering and delivery options.

So why settle for a mediocre grocery shopping experience when you can have an exceptional one at our store? Come visit us today and discover a world of fresh and delicious possibilities!

ADVERTISEMENT FOR A BOOK STORE

Looking for a place to explore new ideas, expand your knowledge, and find inspiration? Look no further than our book store!

Our book store is a treasure trove of books and knowledge, offering a vast selection of titles covering every topic and genre imaginable. Whether you're looking for a thrilling mystery novel, a thought-provoking work of non-fiction, or a captivating children's book, we've got something for everyone.

But our book store is more than just a place to buy books. It's a welcoming community hub where people can gather to share ideas, discover new perspectives, and connect with like-minded individuals. From author readings and book clubs to writing workshops and literary events, there's always something happening at our store.

At our book store, we're passionate about books and the power they have to transform lives. We believe that books can change the world, one reader at a time. That's why we're committed to providing a space where people can come together to learn, grow, and explore the world around them.

Our knowledgeable staff are always on hand to offer recommendations, answer questions, and help you find the perfect book to suit your interests. And with our comfortable seating areas and cozy atmosphere, our store is the perfect place to relax and lose yourself in a good book.

So why not visit our book store today and discover a new world of ideas and inspiration? We're confident that you'll find something that speaks to you and leaves a lasting impact on your life.

ADVERTISEMENT FOR A BAKERY

Looking for a delicious treat that's guaranteed to satisfy your sweet tooth? Look no further than our bakery shop!

Our bakery is a haven for anyone who loves the taste of freshly baked goods. From soft and flaky croissants to rich and decadent cakes, our bakery offers a wide selection of delicious treats that are sure to delight your taste buds.

But it's not just the taste that sets our bakery apart. We take pride in using only the finest and freshest ingredients, ensuring that every bite of our baked goods is a heavenly experience. Our skilled bakers use traditional techniques to create authentic and artisanal treats that are bursting with flavor and texture.

At our bakery, we believe that food should be a celebration of life and that every bite should be savored and enjoyed. That's why we offer a range of products to suit every occasion, from elegant wedding cakes and custom birthday cakes to simple and satisfying pastries and breads.

And with our commitment to quality and customer service, you can trust that you're getting the very best when you shop at our bakery. Our friendly and knowledgeable staff are always on hand to offer recommendations, answer questions, and ensure that you have a truly enjoyable shopping experience.

So why settle for a bland and boring dessert when you can indulge in a truly exceptional one at our bakery shop? Come visit us today and treat yourself to something truly special!

ADVERTISEMENT FOR A SUPERMARKET

Looking for a convenient and affordable way to stock up on all your household essentials? Look no further than our supermarket!

Our supermarket offers a wide selection of products at affordable prices, making it easy to find everything you need in one convenient location. From fresh produce and meats to pantry staples and cleaning supplies, we've got you covered with a comprehensive range of high-quality products.

But it's not just the wide selection and low prices that make our supermarket special. We pride ourselves on our commitment to customer service and satisfaction, with a team of friendly and knowledgeable staff always on hand to offer advice and assistance.

And with our commitment to quality and sustainability, you can feel good about the products you're buying. We work closely with suppliers and farmers to ensure that our products are fresh, healthy, and responsibly sourced, and we're constantly seeking out new and innovative products to add to our shelves.

At our supermarket, we believe that shopping should be an enjoyable and stress-free experience. That's why we offer a range of services and amenities to make your visit as convenient and enjoyable as possible, including online ordering and delivery, in-store cafes and delis, and easy-to-navigate aisles and displays.

So why settle for a mediocre shopping experience when you can have an exceptional one at our supermarket? Come visit us today and discover a world of high-quality products and unbeatable value!

ADVERTISEMENT FOR A MALL

Looking for a one-stop-shop for all your shopping needs? Look no further than our mall!

Our mall is a shopper's paradise, offering a comprehensive range of stores and services that cater to all tastes and budgets. Whether you're looking for high-end fashion, home decor, electronics, or anything in between, you'll find it all under one roof at our mall.

But it's not just the wide selection of stores that makes our mall special. We've designed our mall with the customer in mind, with a range of amenities and services to make your visit as enjoyable and convenient as possible. From comfortable seating areas and free Wi-Fi to clean and well-maintained restrooms, we've thought of everything to ensure that your shopping experience is a pleasant one.

And with our commitment to quality and customer service, you can trust that you're getting the very best when you shop at our mall. Our friendly and knowledgeable staff are always on hand to offer advice and assistance, and we're constantly seeking out new and innovative products and services to add to our offerings.

But it's not just about shopping at our mall. We believe that shopping should be an experience, and that's why we offer a range of entertainment options and events to make your visit even more enjoyable. From movie theaters and restaurants to live music and cultural festivals, there's always something exciting happening at our mall.

So why settle for a mundane shopping experience when you can have an unforgettable one at our mall? Come visit us today and discover a world of shopping, entertainment, and excitement!

ADVERTISEMENT FOR A THEATER

Looking for an escape from the stresses of everyday life? Look no further than our theater!

Our theater is a haven for anyone who loves the magic of live performances. From Broadway hits and classic plays to musicals and experimental productions, we offer a wide range of shows that are sure to delight and inspire.

But it's not just the quality of the performances that makes our theater special. We believe that going to the theater should be an experience, and that's why we go above and beyond to create a welcoming and immersive environment for our guests. From comfortable seating and state-of-the-art sound and lighting to spacious lobbies and bars, we've thought of everything to ensure that your visit is an enjoyable and memorable one.

And with our commitment to quality and customer service, you can trust that you're getting the very best when you attend a show at our theater. Our staff are passionate and knowledgeable about the arts, and we're always happy to offer recommendations and answer any questions you may have.

But it's not just about the shows at our theater. We believe that the arts have the power to enrich our lives and transform our communities, and that's why we're committed to supporting local artists and organizations. We work closely with community groups and cultural institutions to provide opportunities for emerging artists and to foster a vibrant and diverse arts scene in our city.

So why settle for a mundane evening when you can have a thrilling and unforgettable experience at our theater? Come visit us today and discover the magic of live performance!

ADVERTISEMENT FOR A CINEMA HALL

Looking for a thrilling and immersive movie-watching experience? Look no further than our cinema hall!

Our cinema hall offers a state-of-the-art facility with cutting-edge technology that guarantees an exceptional viewing experience. Our large screens and high-quality sound system ensure that you're fully immersed in the action, bringing your favorite movies to life like never before.

But it's not just the technology that makes our cinema hall special. We've designed our space with the customer in mind, with comfortable seating, spacious aisles, and clean and well-maintained restrooms. Our friendly and knowledgeable staff are always on hand to assist you with any questions or concerns, and we're committed to making sure that your visit is an enjoyable and stress-free one.

And with our commitment to quality and customer service, you can trust that you're getting the very best when you come to our cinema hall. We carefully curate our movie selection to include a diverse range of genres and styles, ensuring that there's something for everyone. And with our competitive pricing and regular promotions, you can enjoy a thrilling movie-watching experience without breaking the bank.

But it's not just about the movies at our cinema hall. We believe that the movies have the power to bring people together and inspire new perspectives, and that's why we're committed to supporting local artists and organizations. We regularly host film festivals and special screenings that celebrate diverse perspectives and promote a thriving arts scene in our community.

So why settle for a lackluster movie-watching experience when you can have an exceptional one at our cinema hall? Come visit us today and discover the thrill of the movies!

ADVERTISEMENT FOR A TOY STORE

Looking for a place to spark your child's imagination and bring joy to their playtime? Look no further than our toy store!

Our toy store is a haven for anyone who loves the wonder and magic of toys. From classic board games and puzzles to action figures and dolls, we offer a wide range of toys that are sure to delight and inspire children of all ages.

But it's not just the variety of toys that makes our store special. We believe that the best toys are those that engage a child's imagination and encourage creativity, and that's why we carefully curate our selection to include toys that are not only fun but also educational and developmentally appropriate.

And with our commitment to quality and customer service, you can trust that you're getting the very best when you shop at our toy store. Our staff are passionate about toys and children's development, and we're always happy to offer recommendations and answer any questions you may have.

But it's not just about the toys at our store. We believe that play is an essential part of childhood, and that's why we're committed to supporting local organizations and programs that promote play and child development. We regularly donate toys to children's hospitals and community centers, and we work closely with local schools and educators to provide resources and support for children's learning and development.

So why settle for a mundane toy-buying experience when you can have a thrilling and enriching one at our toy store? Come visit us today and discover the magic of play!

ADVERTISEMENT FOR A FUN ZONE

Looking for a place where your kids can have a blast and burn off some energy? Look no further than our fun zone for kids!

Our fun zone is designed with kids in mind, with a wide range of activities and games that are sure to keep them entertained for hours. From climbing walls and obstacle courses to arcade games and laser tag, we offer a variety of exciting and engaging experiences that will delight children of all ages.

But it's not just about the fun and games at our fun zone. We believe in creating an environment that is safe, clean, and welcoming for children and families. Our staff are trained to prioritize safety and ensure that all equipment and activities are properly maintained and supervised. We also offer a variety of snacks and refreshments to keep kids fueled and hydrated during their playtime.

And with our commitment to quality and customer service, you can trust that you're getting the very best when you come to our fun zone. We pride ourselves on providing a positive and memorable experience for every child and family that visits us. Our staff are friendly and knowledgeable, and we're always happy to answer any questions or provide assistance whenever needed.

But it's not just about the kids at our fun zone. We believe in giving back to our community and supporting local organizations that promote children's well-being and development. We regularly host fundraising events and donate a portion of our proceeds to charities and non-profits that focus on children's health, education, and welfare.

So why settle for a boring and mundane day when you can have an exciting and memorable one at our fun zone for kids? Come visit us today and let your kids unleash their inner thrill-seekers!

ARGUMENTATIVE WRITING

SHOULD STUDENTS BE REQUIRED TO WEAR UNIFORMS IN SCHOOL?

Introduction

School uniforms have been a topic of debate for years. Some people believe that uniforms promote equality, while others argue that they suppress individuality. I firmly believe that students should be required to wear uniforms in school for several reasons.

Promote Unity and Equality

Wearing school uniforms can promote a sense of unity and equality among students. When everyone is dressed the same, there is no competition to wear the latest fashion or designer clothes. This can create a level playing field where everyone is equal, regardless of their socioeconomic background. In addition, school uniforms can help to create a sense of belonging and pride in the school community.

Reduce Bullying

Another benefit of school uniforms is that they can help to

reduce bullying. When everyone is dressed the same, there is less opportunity to make fun of someone's clothing. This can help to create a more inclusive and supportive school environment. In addition, uniforms can eliminate the pressure to wear certain clothes to fit in with a particular social group.

Improve Focus on Learning

School uniforms can also improve the focus on learning in the classroom. When students are dressed in appropriate attire, it can help to create a more professional and serious atmosphere. This can help to reduce distractions and promote a better learning environment.

Increasing Safety

School uniforms can also increase safety in schools. When everyone is dressed in the same clothing, it can be easier to identify who belongs in the school and who does not. This can help to prevent strangers from entering the school unnoticed. In addition, uniforms can eliminate the use of gang colors or symbols, which can help to reduce gang activity.

Conclusion

In conclusion, there are several benefits to requiring students to wear uniforms in school. They can promote unity and equality, reduce bullying, improve focus on learning, and increase safety in schools. While individuality and self-expression are important, they can still be expressed through other means such as accessories or hairstyles. Ultimately, school uniforms can help to create a more positive and inclusive learning environment for all students.

SHOULD STUDENTS BE REQUIRED TO WEAR UNIFORMS IN SCHOOL?

Introduction

The issue of whether or not students should be required to wear uniforms in school has been a topic of debate for many years. While some argue that uniforms promote a sense of community and help to reduce distractions in the classroom, I believe that students should not be required to wear uniforms in school.

Individual Expression

Uniforms can limit students' ability to express their individuality and creativity. Students should have the right to express themselves through their clothing choices, and uniforms can restrict this form of self-expression. By allowing students to dress in their own unique styles, they are able to develop a sense of personal identity and confidence.

Financial Burden

Uniforms can also be a financial burden on families, particularly those with multiple children in school. Uniforms can be expensive, and families may struggle to afford them. This can create inequalities among students, as some may not be able to afford the required uniforms and may feel embarrassed or excluded as a result.

Ineffective Addressing Behavior Issues

Uniforms are often touted as a way to reduce distractions in the classroom and to address behavior issues. However, research has shown that uniforms have little to no impact on academic achievement or student behavior. Addressing these issues requires more comprehensive approaches, such as effective classroom management and addressing the root causes of behavior issues.

No Clear Educational Benefits

There is no clear evidence that uniforms have any educational benefits. While some may argue that uniforms promote a sense of community and school spirit, these can be fostered through other means, such as extracurricular activities and school-wide events.

Conclusion

In conclusion, students should not be required to wear uniforms in school, as uniforms can limit individual expression, be a financial burden on families, and have little to no impact on behavior issues or academic achievement. It is important to consider the well-being and individuality of each student, and to create a learning environment that promotes personal expression and confidence.

SHOULD HOMEWORK BE BANNED IN SCHOOLS?

Introduction

Homework has been a staple of the education system for many years, but there is ongoing debate about whether it is truly beneficial for students. In my opinion, homework should be banned in schools for several reasons.

Reduce Stress

One of the main reasons homework should be banned is that it can cause undue stress on students. Homework often adds to the workload that students have to manage, and it can become overwhelming, especially when students have multiple assignments due at the same time. This can lead to anxiety and even physical health problems.

Promote Learning in the Classroom

Another reason to ban homework is that it can take away from the time students have to learn in the classroom. When students are given too much homework, they may not have enough time to fully understand the material covered in class. This can lead to frustration and a lack of interest in learning.

Allow for Other Activities

Banning homework would also allow students to participate in other activities outside of school. Many students have after-school activities or part-time jobs that they cannot fully commit to because of homework assignments. Without homework, students would have more time to pursue other interests and develop important life skills.

Reduce Inequality

Homework can also create an unequal playing field for students. Some students may have more resources or support at home to complete assignments, while others may not. This can lead to unfair grades and a lack of equal opportunities for all students.

Conclusion

In conclusion, homework should be banned in schools. It can cause stress, take away from classroom learning, limit opportunities for other activities, and create inequality among students. There are other ways for students to learn and practice their skills outside of the classroom, such as through project-based learning or reading assignments. Ultimately, by banning homework, we can create a more positive and inclusive learning environment for all students.

SHOULD HOMEWORK BE BANNED IN SCHOOLS?

Introduction

Homework has long been a controversial topic in education, with some arguing that it is essential for student learning and development, while others argue that it is unnecessary and even harmful. However, I believe that homework should not be banned in schools, for several reasons.

Reinforcement of Learning

Homework provides an opportunity for students to reinforce and apply what they have learned in class. Completing homework assignments can help students to solidify their understanding of key concepts, and can also help them to develop important skills such as time management and self-discipline.

Preparation for College and Career

Homework also helps to prepare students for the demands of college and the workforce, where independent learning and self-motivation are essential skills. By completing homework assignments, students develop the ability to manage their time effectively and to take responsibility for their own learning.

Equal Opportunity

Banning homework could create inequalities in academic achievement among students, as those who have access to resources and support at home may have an advantage over those who do not. Homework provides a level playing field for all students, regardless of their home life or socio-economic status.

Parental Involvement

Homework can also provide an opportunity for parents to be involved in their child's education. By helping their children with homework, parents can stay informed about their child's progress and provide additional support and guidance as needed.

Conclusion

In conclusion, homework should not be banned in schools, as it provides an opportunity for students to reinforce their learning, develop important skills, and prepare for college and career. Homework also promotes equal opportunity and parental involvement in education. While there may be concerns about the amount and type of homework assigned, it is important to consider the benefits of homework and to work towards finding a balance that supports student learning and well-being.

SHOULD ALL STUDENTS BE REQUIRED TO LEARN A SECOND LANGUAGE IN SCHOOL?

Introduction

Learning a second language has become increasingly important in our globalized world. Some argue that it should be a requirement for all students to learn a second language in school. In my opinion, I strongly believe that all students should be required to learn a second language for several reasons.

Increase Opportunities

Learning a second language can increase opportunities for students. In today's job market, many employers prefer or require candidates who are bilingual or multilingual. Additionally, being able to speak a second language can open doors for international travel, studying abroad, and connecting with people from different cultures.

Improve Brain Function

Studies have shown that learning a second language can improve brain function. It can enhance cognitive abilities such as memory, problem-solving, and creativity. Additionally, it can delay the onset of cognitive decline in later life.

Promote Cultural Understanding

Learning a second language can also promote cultural understanding and empathy. When students learn a new language, they also learn about the culture and customs of the people who speak it. This can help to break down barriers and foster respect for other cultures.

Better Communication

Being able to speak a second language can also improve communication skills. It can help students to better understand and express themselves, as well as communicate with a wider range of people. This can be especially beneficial in diverse communities and international settings.

Conclusion

In conclusion, all students should be required to learn a second language in school. It can increase opportunities, improve brain function, promote cultural understanding, and enhance communication skills. By learning a second language, students can become global citizens who are better equipped to navigate our interconnected world.

SHOULD ALL STUDENTS BE REQUIRED TO LEARN A SECOND LANGUAGE IN SCHOOL?

Introduction

In recent years, there has been an increasing emphasis on the importance of learning a second language, with many schools now requiring students to study a foreign language. However, I believe that not all students should be required to learn a second language in school for several reasons.

Lack of Interest and Motivation

Not all students are interested in or motivated to learn a second language. For some students, learning a second language may feel like a chore or an obligation, and may not be a meaningful or enjoyable experience. This can lead to decreased engagement and a lack of progress in language learning.

Limited Resources and Time

Learning a second language requires significant resources and time, including qualified teachers, materials, and classroom time. Schools may not have the resources to adequately support language learning for all students, and may need to prioritize other academic subjects that are considered more essential for student success.

Individual Needs and Abilities

Each student is unique and may have different needs and abilities when it comes to language learning. For some students, learning a second language may be too challenging or may not align with their strengths and interests. It may be more beneficial for these students to focus on other subjects that are better suited to their needs and abilities.

Opportunity Cost

There is an opportunity cost to requiring all students to learn a second language. The time and resources devoted to language learning could be used to support other academic subjects or extracurricular activities that may be more relevant or beneficial for students.

Conclusion

In conclusion, not all students should be required to learn a second language in school. For some students, language learning may not be a meaningful or enjoyable experience, and schools may not have the resources to adequately support language learning for all students. It is important to consider individual needs and abilities when making decisions about language learning, and to prioritize resources and time for academic subjects and activities that are most relevant and beneficial for students.

SHOULD PARENTS LIMIT THEIR CHILDREN'S SCREEN TIME?

Introduction

Screen time has become an increasingly prevalent part of children's lives in recent years, with many parents and educators concerned about the potential negative effects on children's health and development. However, I believe that parents should not necessarily limit their children's screen time, for several reasons.

Access to Information and Learning Opportunities

Screen time can provide children with access to a wealth of information and learning opportunities that may not be available through other means. Educational apps, online resources, and interactive games can help children to develop a wide range of skills, from problem-solving and critical thinking to reading and writing.

Social Interaction

Screen time can also provide children with opportunities for social interaction, particularly in today's digital age. Online communities and multiplayer games can help children to connect with others who share their interests, and may provide a sense of belonging and social support.

Balance and Moderation

Rather than limiting screen time outright, parents can teach their children about balance and moderation when it comes to screen time. Encouraging children to take breaks, engage in physical activity, and participate in other non-screen-based activities can help to promote healthy habits and reduce the potential negative effects of excessive screen time.

Individual Differences

It is also important to consider that each child is unique and may have different needs and preferences when it comes to screen time. Some children may benefit from more screen time than others, depending on their interests, learning styles, and social needs.

Conclusion

In conclusion, parents should not necessarily limit their children's screen time, as it can provide access to information, learning opportunities, and social interaction. However, it is important for parents to promote balance and moderation when it comes to screen time, and to consider individual differences among children. By doing so, parents can help to ensure that their children are engaging in healthy habits and developing the skills and knowledge needed for success in today's digital world.

SHOULD PARENTS LIMIT THEIR CHILDREN'S SCREEN TIME?

Introduction

In today's digital age, children are spending more and more time in front of screens, whether it be smartphones, tablets, computers, or televisions. Some parents believe that they should limit their children's screen time, while others argue that it is not necessary. In my opinion, parents should limit their children's screen time for several reasons.

Promote Health and Well-being

First and foremost, limiting screen time can promote the health and well-being of children. Excessive screen time has been linked to a number of negative health outcomes, including obesity, sleep disturbances, and eye strain. By limiting screen time, parents can help their children maintain a healthy lifestyle.

Encourage Physical Activity

Limiting screen time can also encourage children to engage in physical activity. When children spend less time in front of screens, they have more time to play, exercise, and participate in outdoor activities. This can lead to improved physical health, as well as social and emotional development.

Improve Academic Performance

Too much screen time can also have a negative impact on academic performance. When children spend hours on screens, they may have difficulty concentrating, retaining information, and completing schoolwork. By limiting screen time, parents can help their children to focus on their studies and perform better in school.

Promote Family Time

Limiting screen time can also promote family time and strengthen relationships. When children and parents spend time together without screens, they can engage in meaningful conversations, play games, and create lasting memories. This can help to build strong bonds and foster a sense of belonging within the family.

Conclusion

In conclusion, parents should limit their children's screen time for the sake of their health and well-being, academic performance, and family relationships. It is important to find a balance between screen time and other activities, and to set clear rules and boundaries for children. By doing so, parents can help their children lead healthy and fulfilling lives.

SHOULD THERE BE EXAMINATIONS IN SCHOOL?

Introduction

Examinations have been a part of the education system for centuries, with the aim of evaluating a student's knowledge and understanding of a particular subject. However, there has been an ongoing debate about the effectiveness of examinations in schools. In my opinion, there should be examinations in schools for several reasons.

Measure Student's Progress

Examinations provide a clear way of measuring a student's progress in a particular subject. They can help teachers to identify areas where students may be struggling and provide additional support and resources to help them improve. This can ultimately lead to better academic outcomes for students.

Encourage Learning

Examinations can also encourage learning and motivate students to study and prepare for their exams. When students have a clear goal to work towards, they are more likely to engage with the material and take their studies seriously. This can lead to better retention of information and a deeper understanding of the subject.

Prepare for Future

Examinations also prepare students for the future. In many professions, such as medicine, law, and engineering, individuals are required to take licensing or certification exams to demonstrate their knowledge and competence. By taking exams in school, students can develop the skills and strategies needed to succeed in these future endeavors.

Standardization

Examinations can also provide a standardized way of evaluating students across different schools and regions. This can help to ensure that all students are held to the same academic standards and are prepared for higher education or the workforce.

Conclusion

In conclusion, there should be examinations in schools for the purpose of measuring student progress, encouraging learning, preparing for the future, and providing a standardized way of evaluation. While exams may be stressful for some students, they are an important part of the education system and can ultimately lead to better outcomes for students. It is important, however, for teachers and educators to ensure that exams are fair, balanced, and reflective of the material covered in class

SHOULD THERE BE EXAMINATIONS IN SCHOOL?

Introduction

Examinations have been a part of the education system for centuries, but there is a growing argument against the effectiveness of exams in schools. In my opinion, there should not be examinations in schools for several reasons.

Stress and Anxiety

Examinations can be a significant source of stress and anxiety for many students. The pressure to perform well and the fear of failure can lead to a number of negative outcomes, including decreased self-esteem, mental health problems, and even physical illness. This can ultimately have a negative impact on a student's academic performance and well-being.

Narrow Focus

Examinations often focus on a narrow range of skills and knowledge, which may not accurately reflect a student's overall abilities and strengths. This can lead to a limited understanding of a subject, and may not fully prepare students for real-world situations where critical thinking, problem-solving, and creativity are necessary.

Cheating and Inequality

Examinations can also promote cheating and inequality among students. Those who have access to resources such as tutors or study materials may have an unfair advantage over their peers who may not have access to these resources. Additionally, students who cheat on exams may not have a true understanding of the subject matter, and may be ill-prepared for future academic or professional endeavors.

Alternative Assessment Methods

There are alternative assessment methods that can be used instead of exams, such as projects, presentations, and group work. These methods allow students to demonstrate their understanding of a subject in a more comprehensive and meaningful way, and can better reflect a student's abilities and strengths.

Conclusion

In conclusion, there should not be examinations in schools due to the negative impact they can have on student well-being, their narrow focus, the potential for cheating and inequality, and the availability of alternative assessment methods. It is important for educators and schools to consider the long-term effects of exams on students and explore alternative assessment methods that can more accurately reflect a student's abilities and strengths.

SHOULD SCHOOLS HAVE LONGER RECESS PERIODS?

Introduction

As a student, I have always enjoyed recess as it gives me a break from classwork and allows me to socialize and have fun with my friends. However, many schools have been reducing the length of recess periods in recent years. I strongly believe that schools should have longer recess periods, and in this persuasive text, I will explain why.

Body

Firstly, longer recess periods would give students a much-needed break from academic work. After sitting in class and learning for hours, students need time to recharge and refresh their minds. A longer recess period would provide them with the opportunity to relax and clear their minds, which would improve their focus and concentration when they return to class.

Secondly, longer recess periods would encourage physical activity among students. With many students spending hours each day sitting and learning, physical activity is important for their overall health and wellbeing. A longer recess period would give students more time to be active and participate in sports and other physical activities, which would help them stay healthy and active.

Finally, longer recess periods would also provide students with social benefits. During recess, students have the opportunity to socialize and make new friends. With longer recess periods, students would have more time to interact with each other, which would improve their social skills and help them form lasting friendships.

Conclusion

In conclusion, longer recess periods are important for students' physical, mental, and social wellbeing. A longer recess period would provide students with the opportunity to take a break from academic work, engage in physical activity, and socialize with their peers. Therefore, I strongly believe that schools should have longer recess periods to benefit the overall health and wellbeing of their students.

SHOULD SCHOOLS HAVE LONGER RECESS PERIODS?

Introduction

As a student, I have always enjoyed recess as it gives me a break from classwork and allows me to socialize and have fun with my friends. However, the idea of having longer recess periods in schools has been debated, and I am against this idea. In this persuasive text, I will explain why schools should not have longer recess periods.

Body

Firstly, having longer recess periods would take away valuable learning time from the classroom. With schools having tight schedules and a set amount of time to teach students, longer recess periods would eat into valuable class time, reducing the number of hours that students have to learn. This would be detrimental to their education and would not be fair to students who want to learn and succeed academically.

Secondly, longer recess periods would create safety concerns for students. With more time for recess, students would have a longer period to run around and play, which could lead to accidents and injuries. Additionally, having longer recess periods would make it harder for teachers and school staff to supervise students, creating safety concerns for all students.

Finally, longer recess periods could cause problems with the overall school schedule. With longer recess periods, schools would have to adjust their schedules and make changes to accommodate the extra time. This could create problems with scheduling classes, transportation, and other activities, which would disrupt the overall school day.

Conclusion

In conclusion, longer recess periods would take away valuable learning time from the classroom, create safety concerns for students, and cause problems with the overall school schedule. Therefore, I believe that schools should not have longer recess periods, and instead, should focus on providing students with a well-rounded education that balances both academic work and breaks for physical and mental wellness.

SHOULD EATING CHOCOLATES BE BANNED FROM SCHOOL PREMISES?

Introduction

As a student, I enjoy eating chocolates as a treat during my breaks or after school. However, the question of whether chocolates should be banned from school premises has been debated. In this persuasive text, I will explain why chocolates should not be banned from school premises.

Body

Firstly, chocolates can be a source of happiness and a mood booster for students. After a long and stressful day at school, students deserve to have a small treat to lift their spirits. Chocolates can also be a reward for good behavior or academic achievements, motivating students to do their best.

Secondly, chocolates can have health benefits if consumed in moderation. Dark chocolate, for example, is high in antioxidants, which can help prevent cell damage and lower the risk of diseases. Banning chocolates from school premises would deprive students of these potential health benefits.

Finally, banning chocolates from school premises would not solve the issue of unhealthy eating habits among students. Students may simply find other ways to access chocolates or other unhealthy snacks, such as bringing them from home or buying them off-campus. Instead of a ban, schools should focus on promoting healthy eating habits and providing nutritious snacks and meals in their cafeterias.

Conclusion

In conclusion, banning chocolates from school premises would take away a source of happiness and potential health benefits for students, and may not solve the issue of unhealthy eating habits. Therefore, schools should not ban chocolates, but instead, should focus on promoting healthy eating habits and providing nutritious snacks and meals for students.

SHOULD EATING CHOCOLATES BE BANNED FROM SCHOOL PREMISES?

Introduction

As a student, I believe that eating chocolates should be allowed on school premises. While some argue that chocolates should be banned due to health concerns, I believe that there are several reasons why chocolates should not be banned from school premises.

Body

Firstly, banning chocolates from school premises would not necessarily lead to healthier eating habits. Students may still consume chocolates outside of school, and a ban may not address the root causes of unhealthy eating habits, such as lack of access to healthy food options or insufficient education on nutrition. Therefore, instead of a ban, schools should focus on educating students about healthy eating habits and providing nutritious food options in their cafeterias.

Secondly, chocolates can have positive effects on students' mental health. Eating chocolates can boost mood and reduce stress, which can be particularly beneficial for students during exams or periods of high pressure. Banning chocolates may deprive students of this potential source of stress relief and happiness.

Finally, a ban on chocolates may be difficult to enforce and may create unnecessary tension between students and school staff. It may also lead to a sense of rebellion among students, who may be more likely to seek out chocolates as a forbidden treat.

Conclusion

In conclusion, banning chocolates from school premises may not necessarily lead to healthier eating habits, may deprive students of potential mental health benefits, and may create unnecessary tension and rebellion among students. Instead, schools should focus on educating students about healthy eating habits and providing nutritious food options in their cafeterias. Therefore, chocolates should not be banned from school premises.

Printed in Great Britain
by Amazon

42450765R00036